The Tale of Quita the Rescued Dog

Sarah Padget

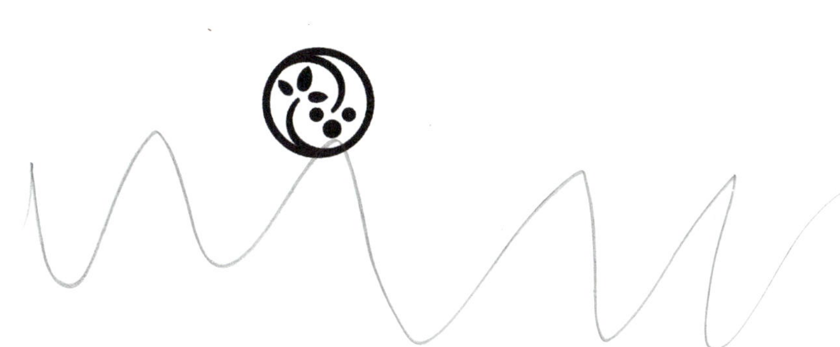

First published 2017
by Rowanvale Books Ltd
Studios 26-28
Meanwhile House Cardiff
Curran Embankment
Cardiff
CF10 5DY
www.rowanvalebooks.com

A CIP catalogue record for this book is available from the British Library.
ISBN: 978-1-911240-55-6

A huge thank you to Mary Allcock for immediately agreeing to illustrate this book for me. It is so heart-warming to know that there are people who will do their utmost to help without any questions.

Thank you, Mary.

'I looked at her through the rusty, twisted wire of the cage.'

We dedicate this book to all those dogs who have been rescued, to all those awaiting rescue and to those who we just haven't found yet... We are coming.

Happy Paws Puppy Rescue
www.happypawspuppyrescue.co.uk
Charity number 1158323

This true tale begins in a country many miles from England called Cyprus, although there are many countries like Cyprus all around the world.

Cyprus is a hot country in the eastern part of the Mediterranean Sea.

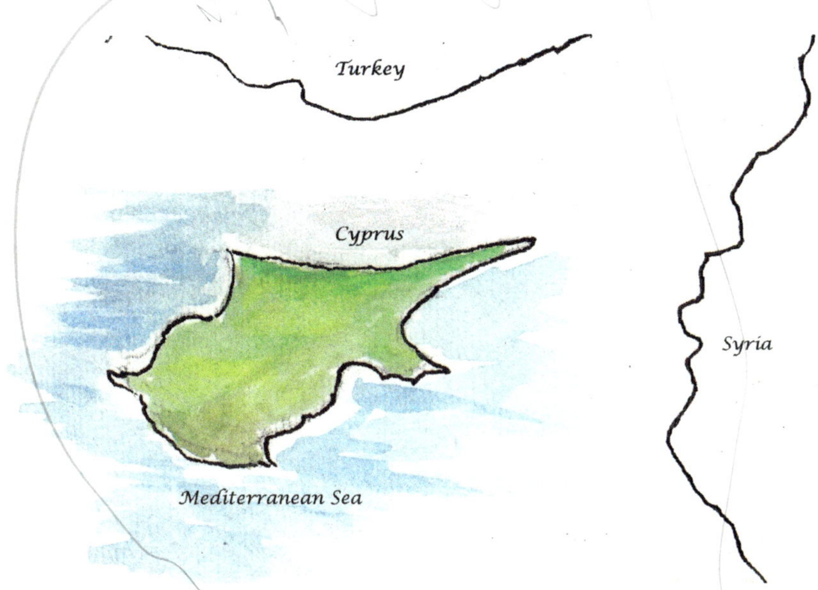

Cyprus has mountains that seem to reach right up into the sky, with snow in winter and soft, cool breezes in the summer. Mountains

with views of towns, villages, farms and the sea.

From the mountains, you can see everything.

My name is Lukas and I am a child, just like you — but I live in Cyprus. One day, I was walking in the mountains when I stopped to gaze in awe at the spectacular view. The mountain path was steep and I was tired and thirsty. I sat on my usual

sun-baked boulder, took out my bottle of refreshing spring water and drank some while enjoying the cool mountain breeze.

In Cyprus, in the summer, you should never go anywhere without a bottle of water to drink.

In the distance, I could see a house down near the town, by the beach. In the back yard I could see a pen — not a very big pen, maybe three paces wide and four paces long.

Shut inside the pen, with no way out, I could see a dog, not very old, lying in the baking sun.

As I sat on the boulder I could see the shimmering heat coming up the mountain towards me. I was glad to be sitting in the cool mountain breeze and not at home in the sticky, stifling heat.

That night, tucked up in my bed, I dreamt of my day on the mountain.

Soon, the puppy who had been shut in the pen crept into my dream.

The next day, the heat forced me to climb the mountains in search of a cool breeze. Again, I could see the dog, the puppy in the pen. I noticed, through the watery, shimmering heat, that the puppy couldn't get out of the sun.

I felt the cool breeze again, blowing across my legs, and shivered a quick shiver.

The dog — the puppy — was panting in the pen. Its water bowl was empty, tipped on its side, with sunlight glinting off the upturned bottom of the shiny metal bowl.

That night, I once again dreamt of the dog — the puppy — trapped in the pen with no shade or water.

A few days later, in the town, the midday heat was cooking the pavements. I saw some boys crowded around in a circle. They seemed to be playing a game. I wanted to join in but the boys were all bigger than me and were unlikely to let me play their rough game.

Instead, I went again to my favourite place, the boulder on the mountain. At least it was cooler and more

peaceful than the hot streets below. I looked over the shimmering town and found myself unconsciously looking for the pen with the puppy, but the puppy was gone.

The pen was empty.

That's strange, I thought, as there was no way out of the pen.

I missed the puppy in the pen with no water or shade.

Later in the afternoon, when the town was cooler, I walked home and again saw the group of boys of twelve or thirteen years old, playing their game of football.

I heard a squeal, then a yelp, then another — louder this time — followed by a frightened whimper. Then I spotted the dog — the puppy — the one that I had watched from the cool boulder on the mountain.

The boys were playing football with the poor puppy. It was not a fun game kicking a ball for the dog to chase; they were using my puppy as the ball.

I could do nothing. I was too young, and if the boys could do that to the puppy, what would they do to me?

I hid and watched in horror, feeling sick.

When the boys had grown tired of

kicking the dog and headed home, and the puppy had crawled away to hide, I ventured cautiously from my hiding place behind the wall.

I stood and listened, and sure enough, I could hear the dog — the puppy — whimpering nearby.

I looked for the puppy then spotted it curled up and very still.

I approached the puppy and ever so gently stroked its back. The puppy

lifted its head to look up at me and weakly wagged its tail. MY puppy seemed to smile at me.

I had to go home — it was late. My puppy followed me, limping and in pain from cuts and bruises on her tummy.

I let the puppy follow me home. Mamá will know what to do, I thought. My mamá always knows what to do.

Although my mamá was kind and felt sorry for the dog, my puppy, who had been imprisoned in a tiny pen with no water and no shade, she said, 'It can't stay with us but I do know someone who can help.'

Mamá telephoned her friend, who came and took my puppy and put her — for it was a little girl — in a pound, which is a temporary home for stray, unloved dogs.

I went to see her after school the next day. I looked at her through the rusty, twisted wire of the cage.

I visited the pound every single day after school, and every single day my puppy whined when she saw me and came to lick my fingers. She was glad to see me.

The puppy was very thin; I could see the outline of her small ribs through her skin. Her tummy was very bruised, black turning to dark red with yellow around the edges. Her skin was covered in ticks that grew fatter as I watched, sucking her blood for their dinner. I gave her a few biscuits and she devoured them gratefully, licking my fingers for the last crumbs.

I felt sad. So sad.

After a few days, the dog — my puppy — was even thinner. She

had a water bowl with water in it but no food.

The man in charge of the pound said, 'She isn't going to be fed. There's no point; she will be put to sleep next week because she is a stray with no owner to look after her.'

I didn't count as an owner. Apparently I was too young.

The next day, my puppy was in the same twisted, rusting cage, but

now she was thinner still. She didn't want to say hello — she didn't even whimper or get up when she saw me.

That afternoon, as I was about to go home, I noticed a different *lady was looking at all the dogs in the pound.*

'I'll take that one, the golden one with black on her ears,' I heard her say.

I was worried; where were they taking my puppy?

The different *lady explained, 'I am going to save the dog from being put to sleep tomorrow.'*

I didn't understand. 'Put to sleep? What does that mean?' I found myself saying out loud. I hadn't meant to say anything.

The different lady didn't want to upset me, but told me that the puppy would be killed because there were too many abandoned, unloved dogs in Cyprus.

'Oh no, she can't be!' I cried.

'Don't worry,' said the different lady, 'I have some friends in England. They want to save the dog, so I will take her to a vet who will look at her tummy, which is very bruised — black turning to dark red with yellow around the edges. The vet will also get rid of the ticks from her body. Then I will give her a meal.'

I felt happier when I heard this — excited, even.

'If you come tomorrow after school, you can see the dog — your puppy.'

The different lady did as she had said she would.

My puppy — the golden one with black on her ears — was so scared, but when I saw her the next day she whimpered, squeaked and wagged her tail. I was so relieved!

She had been to the vet who had removed all the ticks feasting on her blood. The vet had also rubbed some cream onto her tummy to help the bruises, which were now very slowly turning lighter in colour. The vet had said she was lucky not to have any broken ribs; her tummy was still very, very sore.

The puppy had had a warm bath with some special shampoo to help her skin and patchy coat. She had also enjoyed another meaty meal.

Her tail wagged a bit faster and she squeaked a little louder when she saw me. She yawned with a happy, high-pitched whine.

The different lady explained that the dog — my puppy, the golden one with black on her ears and a waggy tail — would stay with her until her English friends could raise enough money for her to travel to England. There she would have her very own family to love her, feed her, play with her and take her for long walks.

I started to cry.

'Thank you,' I sobbed to the different lady.

'I am happy the dog — MY puppy, the golden one with black on her ears and a waggy tail and a high-pitched whine — will be safe and loved and happy.'

Still I cried. I thought of the puppy as mine, and I knew I would miss her when she went to England.

The different lady thought for a moment.

'Would you like to help me get her ready for her new home?' she asked. 'I need to take her to the beach tomorrow. I'm going to take some photos so that her new family can see what she looks like.'

'Yes, please!' I sobbed through happy tears.

The different lady smiled. 'We've decided to call her Quita.' (Which is pronounced 'Key-ta'.)

I beamed and stroked my puppy. 'Hello, little Quita.'

On the beach the next day, we discovered that my puppy, Quita — the golden one with black on her ears and a waggy tail, a high-pitched whine and a cold, black nose — had a passion for seagulls!

Arrangements were soon made to put my puppy, Quita — the golden one with black on her ears and a waggy tail, a high-pitched whine and a cold, black nose and a passion for seagulls — onto an aeroplane.

The different lady's friends in England had put out an appeal and now had enough money for my puppy, Quita — the golden one with black on her ears and a waggy tail, a high-pitched whine and a cold, black nose, a passion for seagulls and a little flesh on her skinny bones — to go to England in one week's time.

I was happy now and couldn't stop smiling; I knew Quita would have a good home, a family to love her, food to eat and plenty of water in a bowl to drink.

I looked after my puppy, Quita —the golden one with black on her ears and a waggy tail, a high pitched whine and a cold, black nose, a passion for seagulls and a little flesh on her skinny bones — every day for that week.

Every day, her tail wagged more and more and more.

The day before she was to go on her big adventure, the different *lady and I treated her to another bath with the special shampoo. She didn't like having a bath and tried so hard to get out. We all got soaked. When we had finished bathing her, it didn't take long for her to dry, running around in the sunshine.*

She had been to the vet again and was now vaccinated and microchipped. She even had her own pet passport and was now fit enough to travel to England.

The different *lady helped me put Quita into her travel crate to see if it was the correct size. It was; Quita had enough room to turn around and a soft blanket to sleep on.*

I explained to my puppy, Quita — the golden one with black on her ears and a waggy tail, a high-pitched whine and a cold, black nose, a passion for seagulls and a little flesh on her skinny bones — what would happen.

She would fly like the birds she loved to chase on the beach, and when she landed in England a family would be there to love her and care for her.

Never again would she be caged without shade under the baking sun. Never again would she be used as a football by cruel boys. Never again would she be scared, starving and alone in a pound, in danger of being put to sleep.

The next day was hot and sunny, as summer always is in Cyprus.

I gave Quita a huge hug and some

kisses, then the *different* lady and I put her in her travel crate, closed the door securely and took her to the aeroplane.

We watched the aeroplane take off. Then, hand in hand, we walked back to the car.

I said to the *different* lady, 'When I grow up I'm going to care for dogs like Quita and find them a good life, just like you do.'

The different lady just nodded, squeezed my hand and drove me home.

I was so happy for the dog,

my puppy called Quita,

the golden one with black on

her ears and a waggy tail,

a high-pitched whine

and a cold, black nose,

a passion for seagulls and a

little flesh on her skinny

bones and now

a forever family and a

loving home in

England.

A Note to the Reader

Quita did indeed come to England, helped by two charities called Dogs Needing Love and Happy Paws Puppy Rescue. There are many such charities carrying out work like this every single day, rescuing dogs and puppies from many countries around the world to give them a chance of life.

This is a true story about Quita, and I am part of her very honoured new family. She is indeed loved and cared for. She has an eleven-year-old golden retriever for a big brother, as well as two cats and six chickens for company. Oh, and a mum and dad who love her very much.

Quita now attends an obedience

class where she is learning new things every day. She really enjoys her agility classes and is so quick to learn. She skilfully runs around the agility course, over jumps, through tunnels and in and out of weaving poles and up and down a seesaw. She has even won rosettes in competitions.

In the evenings, Quita just wants to lie beside a family member. She also likes to lie on laps and nibble ears.

I noticed very quickly that if anybody tries to kick a ball for her to chase, she runs away and cowers. She does the same if somebody picks up a stick, the kitchen broom or the clothes prop.

I take Quita for a walk every morning with her dad, her big brother, Dukey Boy, and her new friends: three Labradors, a Rottweiler, a Spanish Podenco, a large black Great Dane-Doberman crossbreed and a tiny Patterdale terrier. Most of her friends have also been rescued from lives they would not wish to return to.

If you are ever in East Sussex, England, and see a dog — a golden one with black on her ears and a waggy tail, a high-pitched whine and a cold, black nose, a passion for seagulls and a little flesh on her skinny bones and a forever family and a loving home — please remember this true story.

By buying this book, you have helped to rescue another dog just like Quita.

Quita's family and Happy Paws Puppy Rescue thank you for your help.
This is the true tale of Quita, the rescued puppy from Cyprus.

Sarah Padget grew up in Worcestershire in a house with a garden that ran down to the River Severn, but she now lives in rural East Sussex. Sarah trained to make and repair woodwind instruments, but is now a senior karate instructor, along with her partner. They teach karate to both children and adults in Sussex and Kent.

Amongst her hobbies are gardening and looking after her animals. All the animals she and her partner presently own have been rescued from very uncertain lives but now live happily together! Sarah enjoys walking the dogs in the South Downs National Park and local woods. She has recently started training her dog Quita for agility competitions.

www.sarahpadget.com
The Tale of Quita the Rescued Dog - also on Facebook!

Publisher Information

Rowanvale Books provides publishing services to independent authors, writers and poets all over the globe. We deliver a personal, honest and efficient service that allows authors to see their work published, while remaining in control of the process and retaining their creativity. By making publishing services available to authors in a cost-effective and ethical way, we at Rowanvale Books hope to ensure that the local, national and international community benefits from a steady stream of good quality literature.

For more information about us, our authors or our publications, please get in touch.

www.rowanvalebooks.com
info@rowanvalebooks.com

Lightning Source UK Ltd.
Milton Keynes UK
UKOW07f0507161117
312839UK00002B/7/P

9 781911 240556